BIG BOOK OF
BIRD
ILLUSTRATIONS

Selected and Arranged by
MAGGIE KATE

DOVER PUBLICATIONS, INC.
Mineola, New York

DOVER *Pictorial Archive* SERIES

International Standard Book Number: 0-486-41225-3

Manufactured in the United States of America
Dover Publications, Inc., 31 East 2nd Street, Mineola, N.Y. 11501

Publisher's Note

Many birds are identified with various human emotions, and celebrated in myth, poem, and song. Two constellations were given the Latin names Aquila and Cygnus (Eagle and Swan). Eagles and owls also figure in the Greek myths. In Chinese mythology, the appearance of a phoenix indicated the imminence of some great event. The ancient Egyptians adopted the phoenix as part of their ritual of sun-worship, which centered on a variety of heron. The heads of the vulture, falcon, goose, and ibis were used to symbolized several of the major Egyptian gods, both male and female. In more recent times, the Mayan people worshipped the "plumed serpent" god Kulkulcan, who appeared in the later Aztec culture as Quetzalcóatl. The quetzal (a variety of trogon) was the sacred bird of the Mayas. The oral traditions of various Native American groups in North America included creation myths focused on birds, and trickster stories featuring Raven or Crow. In both North and South America, the robin and other locally familiar birds are the focus of tales.

In modern English literature, Shelley's "To a Skylark" and Keats's "Ode to a Nightingale" are among the poems whose appeal has crossed centuries and continents. In the United States, poems using bird imagery have varied from the spare syllables of Emily Dickinson's "A bird came down the walk" to Elizabeth Bishop's "Love is feathered like a bird." Not merely "the bluebird of happiness" and the "red red robin," but even the far-less-familiar titmouse has been featured in song and verse. Birdcalls have been imitated in signal codes, birdsongs reproduced in melodies. In many African cultures, songs associated with birds or with lyrics attributed to them are common. An example is one in which a male nightjar laments the fact that "maidens" are not attracted to him because his features are not handsome. Some of the songs, in several languages, include representations of birdcalls. In South Africa, boys and young men compete to devise the best bird riddles in which a species of bird is likened to a person or to a type of person—such as saying that the white-collared raven is like a missionary.

Birds' feathers of diverse kinds have been used in many times and places for adornment, and also as amulets and in spiritual symbols. Eagle feathers were especially important in the rituals of several North American tribes, notably those who dwelt in the Great Plains. In mythology, folktales, popular songs, nursery rhymes, and opera, birds such as the phoenix, the condor, the raven, the crow, the swan, and the goose have embodied specific attributes. The image of a female bird—or a pair—feeding and protecting nestlings is the height of heartwarmingness, while the profile of a wide-wingspanned bird soaring or powerfully beating the air is emblematic of freedom. On a more mundane level, plucked plumage has been used in quilts, pillows, mattresses, and clothing—for keeping warm—and as fans—for getting cool.

Birds, in astonishing variety (about 8,650 species) and enormous total numbers, are found in every climate on the planet. Almost 800 species are found in the United States and Canada. Colombia is the country that is home to the largest number of bird species—more than 1,700. Small Costa Rica has the largest number of species per square mile, fostering about as many as live in the vast expanse of the United States and Canada combined. The reasons for the great proliferation of bird variety in Colombia and in Costa Rica are that both of these countries of South and Central America have fecund tropical rain forests, a variety of habitats, and several altitude zones, each with vegetation, temperature, and animal life suited for differing bird species.

Fossil records show that most of the species living today have been around for hundreds of thousands of years. Some, as different as ostriches and penguins, are flightless. Others run about on the ground more than they fly. Still others soar above the ocean or float on its surface for months at a time, without ever alighting on land. Most people may not notice the constant presence of birds very much, unless they suddenly are faced with their absence: the harrowing situation predicted by Rachel Carson in her 1962 book *Silent Spring.*

The oldest known fossil bird, dubbed Archaeopteryx ("ancient flying creature") seems to have flourished during the Late Jurassic period and may embody the transition between true birds and their flying reptile ancestors, known as pterodactyls or pterosaurs. This crow-size creature had a mixture of reptilian and avian features: a long tail with 20 vertebrae, 3 toes with claws on each foot, some hollow bones, a small brain, and feathers much like those on the wings of modern birds.

For half a century, the field guides and other writings of ornithologist and artist Roger Tory Peterson, along with his paintings of birds from around the world, have fascinated millions of people. Many other checklists, classifications, and introductory ornithology guides are available for people who want to get started as birdwatchers, or to photograph or draw birds. Any person living in North America can expect to see at least 250 species of birds—and many more, with a little effort—in a lifetime. As a preliminary to getting out and watching birds, or simply to decide which species to get acquainted with, or to find an apt illustration for a project with a bird motif or connection, a perusal of the *Big Book of Bird Illustrations* will give a good introduction to the amazing variety of bill types, wing forms, crests and other elaborations of plumage, toes/talons/claws, nest varieties, sizes, and shapes found in the avian world. Some of the books from which these illustrations were taken, and many birders' books, offer descriptions of habitats, breeding, year-round and winter ranges, migration patterns, calls and songs, coloration, camouflage, diet, predators, mating behavior, eggs, parenting, and all the other elements of boundless bird variation.

Contents

Common Grackle

Mourning Dove

Ruby-Throated
Hummingbird

Northern Bobwhite

Eastern
Wood Pewee

Starling

House Wren

Red-Eyed Vireo

Towhee

Wood Thrush

Eastern Bluebird

Red-Headed Woodpecker

Chimney
Swift

Cedar Waxwing

Blue Jay

Cardinal

Brown
Thrasher

Baltimore
Oriole

Canada Goose

White-Breasted
Nuthatch

Catbird

Brown Creeper

Black-Capped
Chickadee

Barn
Swallow

Nighthawk

Slate-Colored Junco

Mallard

Sparrowhawk

Tufted Titmouse

Robin

Pigeon

Herring Gull

Song Sparrow

Red-Winged
Blackbird

White-Crowned
Sparrow

Common
Yellowthroat

Goldfinch

Yellow-Shafted
Flicker

Common
Crow

Cowbird

Green Heron

House Sparrow

Northern Mockingbird

Killdeer

Downy
Woodpecker

Yellow Warbler

Purple
Martin

Chipping
Sparrow

Myrtle Warbler

Purple
Finch

Belted
Kingfisher

Snowy
Owl

White-Throated
Sparrow

Canada Warbler

Scarlet Tanager

American
Redstart

Painted Bunting

Horned Lark

Robin

Snowy Egret

Whippoorwill

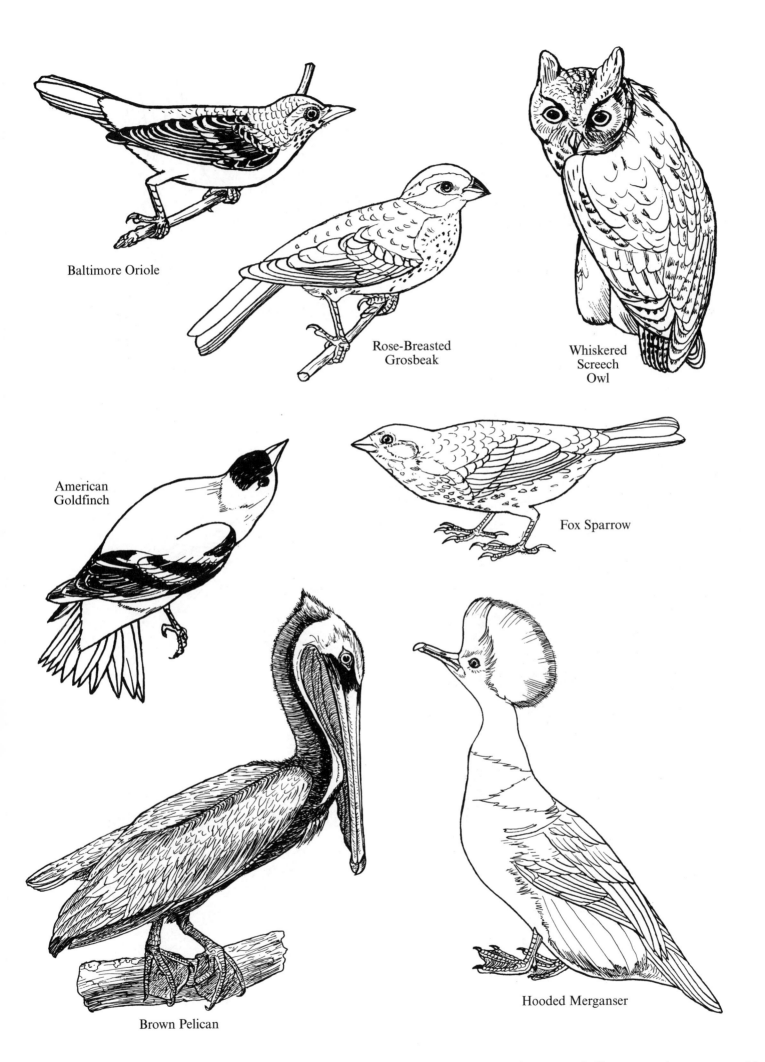

Baltimore Oriole

Rose-Breasted
Grosbeak

Whiskered
Screech
Owl

American
Goldfinch

Fox Sparrow

Brown Pelican

Hooded Merganser

Eastern
Bluebird

Ruby-Throated
Hummingbird

Cardinal

Great Blue
Heron

Eastern Meadowlark

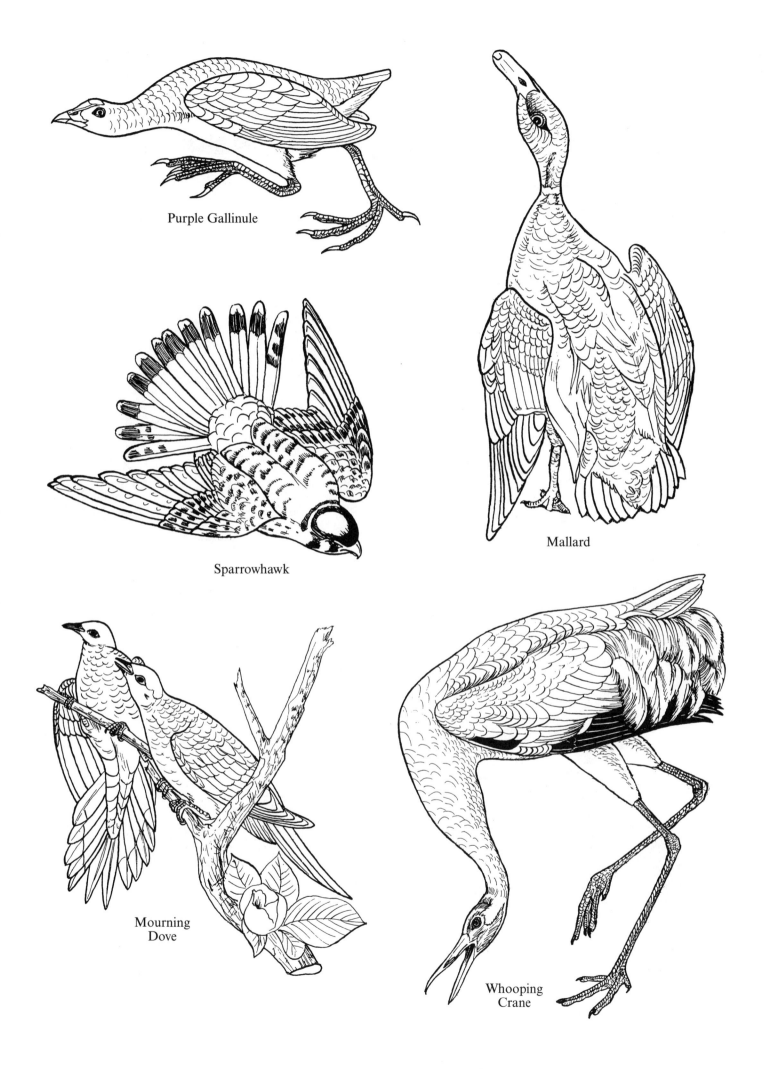

Purple Gallinule

Mallard

Sparrowhawk

Mourning
Dove

Whooping
Crane

Yellow-Breasted Chat

Evening Grosbeak

Rufous-Sided Towhee

Blue Jay

Wild Turkey

Blackburnian Warbler

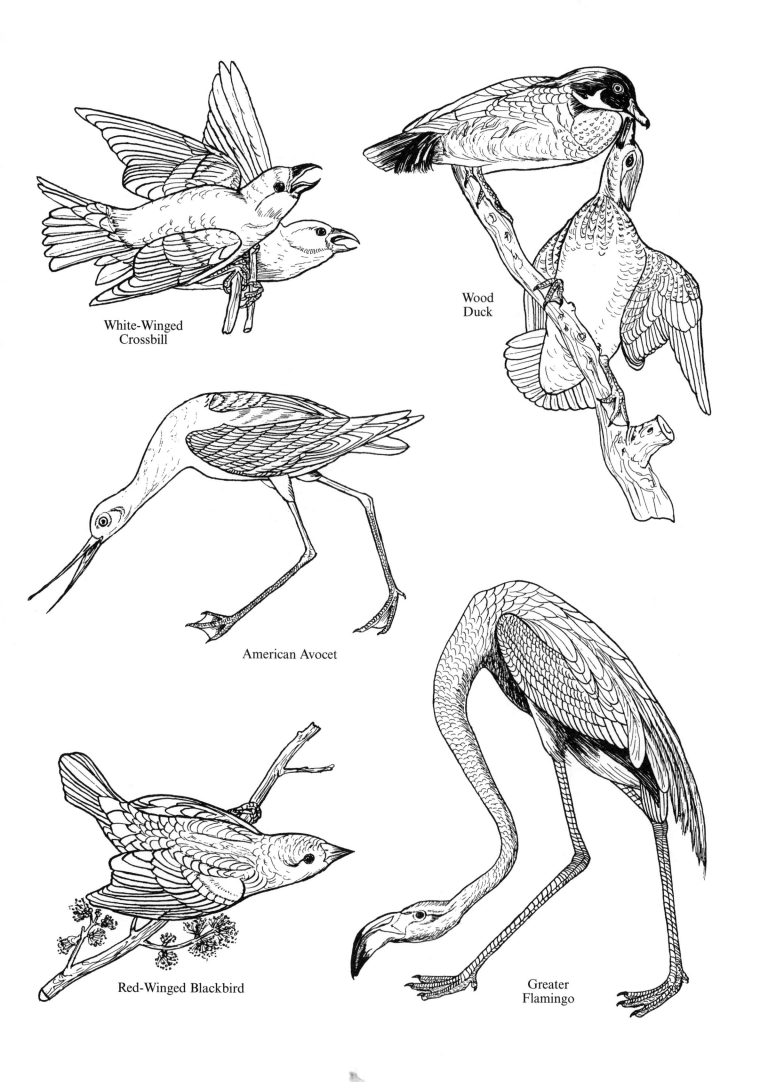

White-Winged
Crossbill

Wood
Duck

American Avocet

Red-Winged Blackbird

Greater
Flamingo

Yellow-Shafted
Flicker

Cerulean Warbler

Chestnut-Sided
Warbler

Pileated Woodpecker

Brown Thrasher

Roseate Spoonbill

Great Gray Owl

Egyptian Vulture

Harpy
Eagle

Ferruginous
Hawk

Common
Black Hawk

Red Kite

African Wood Owl

Red-Tailed
Hawk

Barred Owl

Barn Owl

Short-Eared Owl

Prairie Falcon

Swainson's Hawk

Snowy Owl

Turkey Vulture

Andean Condor

Eastern
Screech Owl

Burrowing Owl

American
Swallow-Tailed Kite

White-Tailed Eagle

Elf Owl

Imperial
Eagle

Osprey

American
Kestrel

Peregrine
Falcon

Snail Kite

Bald
Eagle

Northern
Goshawk

Merlin

Griffon Vulture

Long-Crested
Hawk Eagle

Golden Eagle

Northern
Harrier

Northern
Saw-Whet
Owl

Bateleur

Crested
Caracara

Great
Horned Owl

Sharp-Shinned
Hawk

African
Harrier Hawk

Gray Hawk

Gyrfalcon

Lämmergeier

Yellow-Shafted
Flicker

Cactus Wren

Common Loon

Mountain
Bluebird

Hawaiian Goose or Néné

Lark Bunting

Black-Capped
Chickadee

California Quail

Brown Pelican

American
Goldfinch

Western
Meadowlark

Rhode Island
Red

Willow
Ptarmigan

Northern
Cardinal

Greater
Roadrunner

Baltimore
Oriole

Ruffed Grouse

Bald Eagle

Purple
Finch

Scissor-Tailed
Flycatcher

Carolina
Wren

Hermit
Thrush

American
Robin

Eastern Bluebird

Ring-Necked
Pheasant

Blue Hen
Chicken

Brown
Thrasher

Northern
Mockingbird

California
Gull

Polynesian
Chicken

Hawaiian Owl

White Tern

Crested Honeycreeper

Hawaiian
Gallinule

Hawaiian
Hawk

Northern
Cardinal

Hawaiian
Flycatcher

Hawaiian
Coot

Oahu 'O'o

White-Tailed
Tropicbird

Red-Footed
Booby

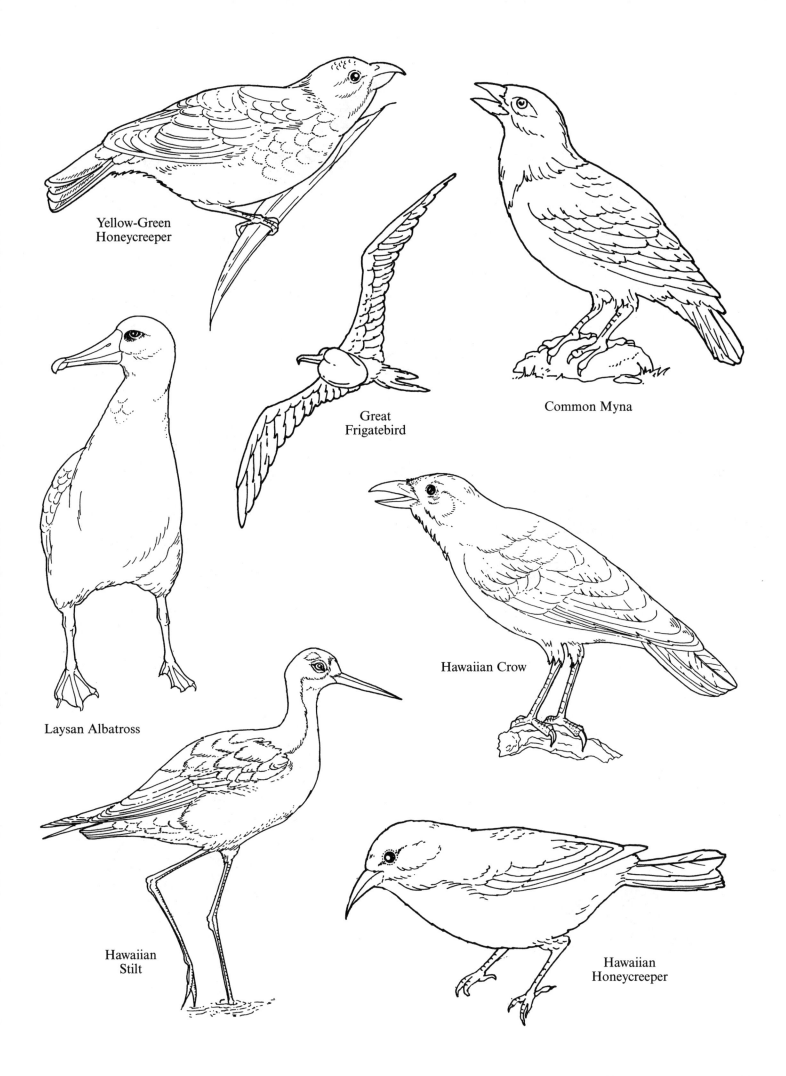

Yellow-Green
Honeycreeper

Great
Frigatebird

Common Myna

Laysan Albatross

Hawaiian Crow

Hawaiian
Stilt

Hawaiian
Honeycreeper

'I'iwi

Hawaiian
Honeycreeper
(small, Kauai variety)

Palila

Hawaiian Duck

Scarlet
Hawaiian
Honeycreeper

Hawaiian Goose
or Néné

Herring Gull

Piping Plover

Magnificent Frigatebird

Dunlin

American Avocet

Great Auk

Black-Necked Stilt

Ruddy Turnstone

Wood
Stork

Long-Billed Curlew

Atlantic
Puffin

Least Sandpiper

Common Snipe

Roseate Spoonbill

Purple Gallinule

Virginia Rail

Northern Gannet

Hooded Merganser

Spectacled Eider

American Oystercatcher

Black-Browed
Albatross

Peregrine
Falcon

Adelie Penguin

Long-Tailed
Jaeger

Limpkin

Wilson's Phalarope

American Coot

Trumpeter Swan

Belted Kingfisher

Double-Crested Cormorant

Great Egret

Brown Pelican

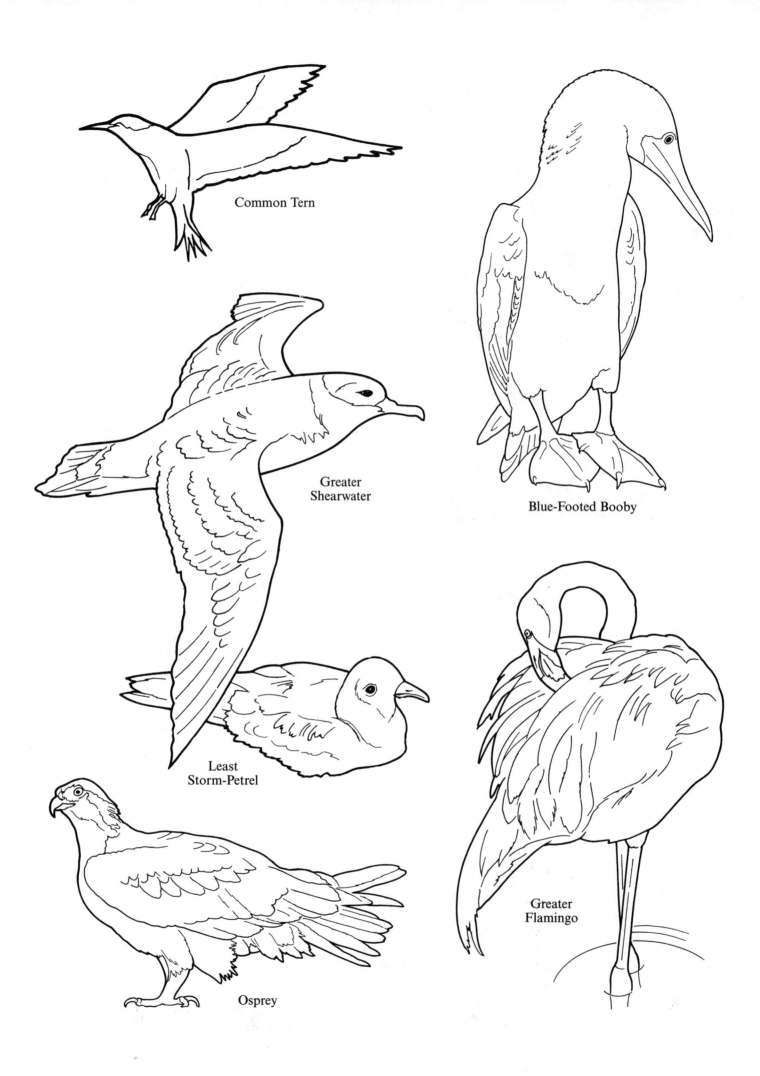

Common Tern

Greater
Shearwater

Blue-Footed Booby

Least
Storm-Petrel

Greater
Flamingo

Osprey

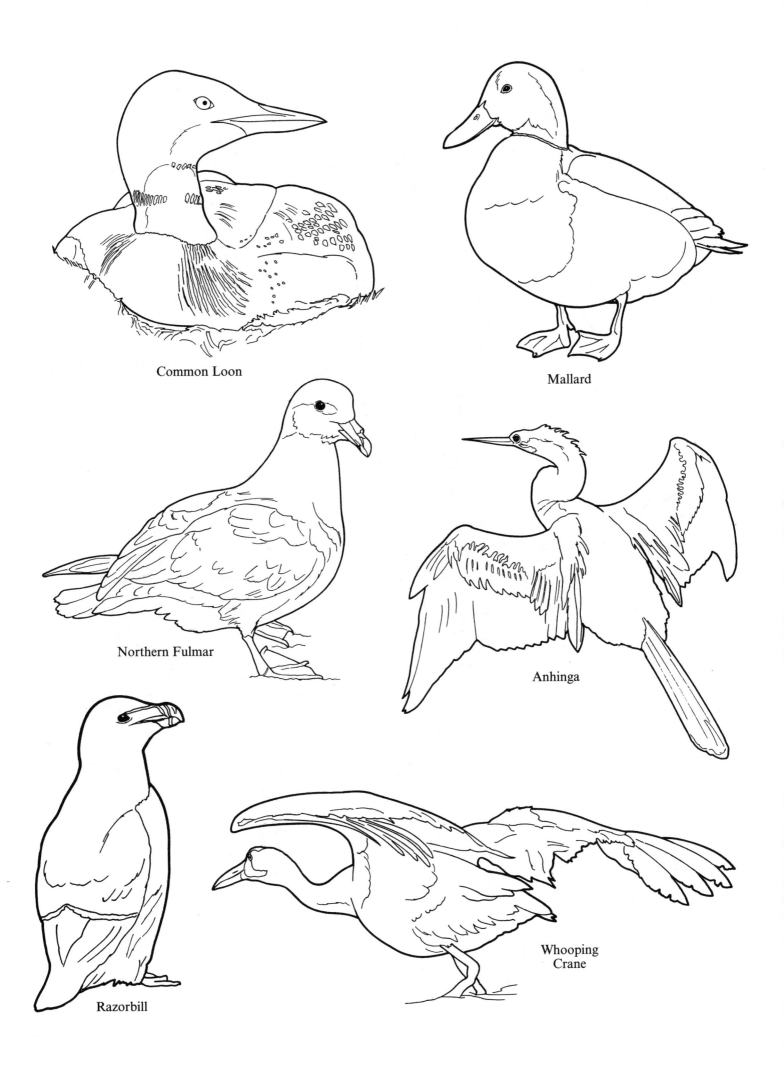

Common Loon

Mallard

Northern Fulmar

Anhinga

Razorbill

Whooping
Crane

Chinstrap Penguin

Gentoo Penguin

Adelie Penguin

Arctic Tern

Emperor Goose

Rockhopper Penguin

Atlantic
Puffin

Gyrfalcon

Black-Browed Albatross

Snowy Owl

Willow Ptarmigan

Black
Guillemot

Emperor Penguin

Skua

Parasitic Jaeger

Wilson's
Storm-Petrel

King Eider

King
Penguin

Lapland
Longspur

Steller's Eider

Wood Duck

King Eider

Mallard

Emperor
Goose

Barrow's Goldeneye

White-Winged Scoter

Snow
Goose

Ross'
Goose

Lesser
Scaup

Greater
White-Fronted
Goose

Hooded Merganser

Ring-Necked Duck

Common
Merganser

Tundra Swan

Surf
Scoter

Fulvous Whistling-Duck

Green-Winged Teal

Common Loon

Black-Bellied
Whistling Duck

Spectacled Eider

Ruddy Duck

Canada
Goose

Cinnamon Teal

Brant

Canvasback

Blue-Winged
Teal

Oldsquaw

American Wigeon

Mute Swan

Common
Shelduck

American Black Duck

Bufflehead

Gadwall

Red-Breasted
Merganser

Barnacle
Goose

Northern Gannet

Common Eider

Harlequin Duck

Greater Scaup

Redhead

Trumpeter Swan

Pileated
Woodpecker

Roseate Spoonbill

Common
Yellowthroat

Wood Stork

King Rail

Green Heron

Barred Owl

Bald Eagle

Marsh Wren

Snowy Egret

Snail Kite

Tricolored Heron

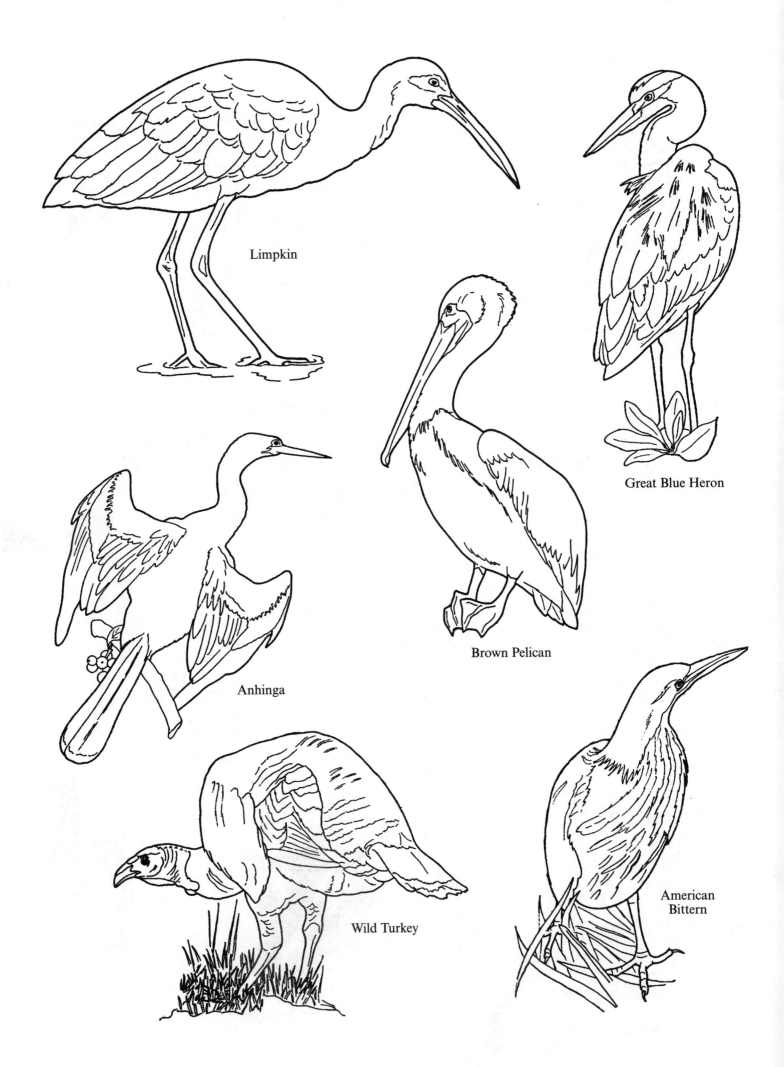

Limpkin

Great Blue Heron

Brown Pelican

Anhinga

Wild Turkey

American
Bittern

'I'iwi

Satin
Bowerbird

Garnet Pitta

Keel-Billed
Toucan

Green
Magpie

Mandarin Duck

Black-Eared
Golden Tanager

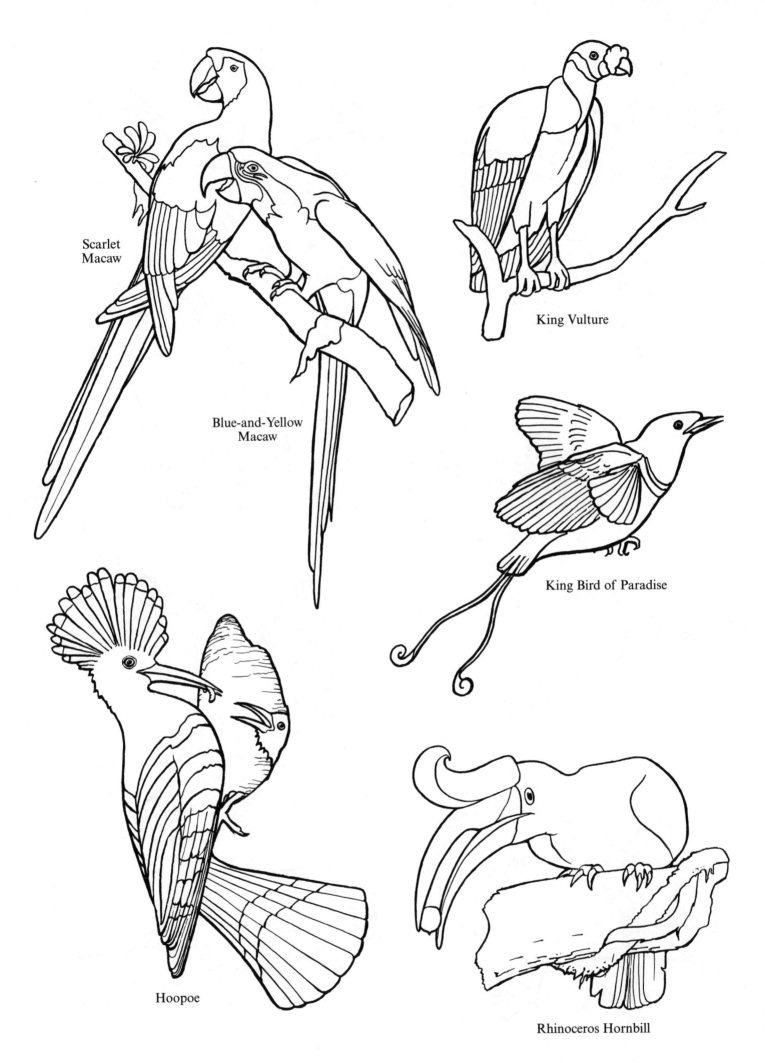

Scarlet
Macaw

Blue-and-Yellow
Macaw

King Vulture

King Bird of Paradise

Hoopoe

Rhinoceros Hornbill

Roseate Spoonbill

Blue Bird of Paradise

Village Weaver

Fairy Bluebird

Sunbittern

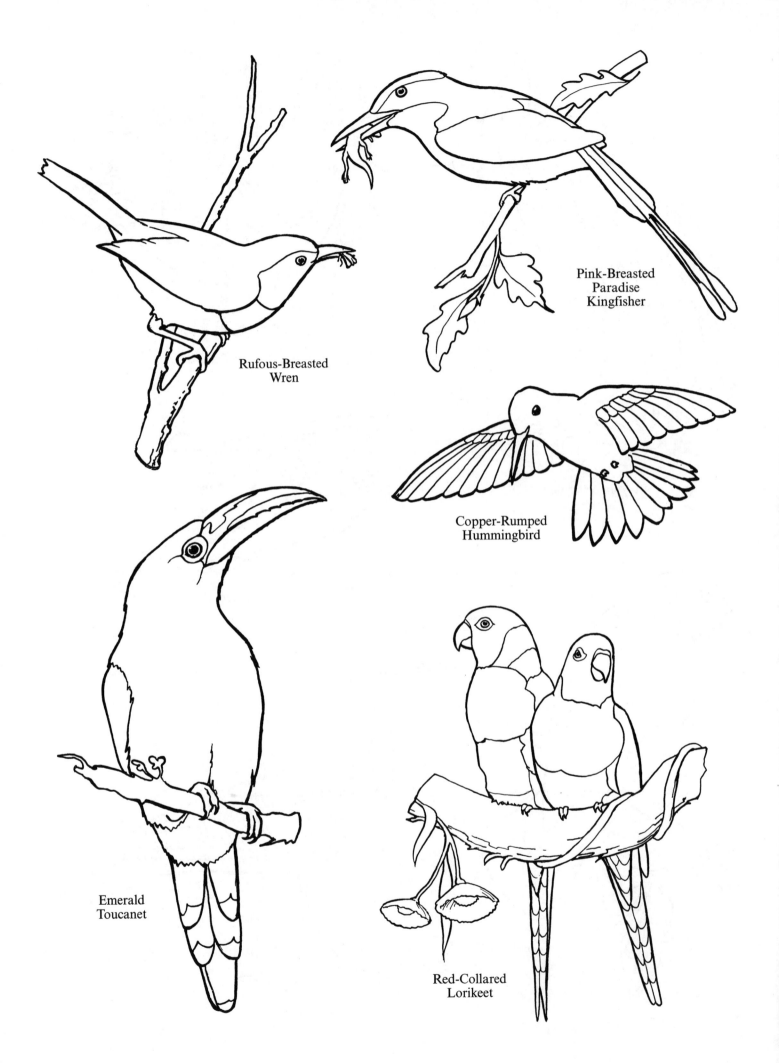

Rufous-Breasted
Wren

Pink-Breasted
Paradise
Kingfisher

Copper-Rumped
Hummingbird

Emerald
Toucanet

Red-Collared
Lorikeet

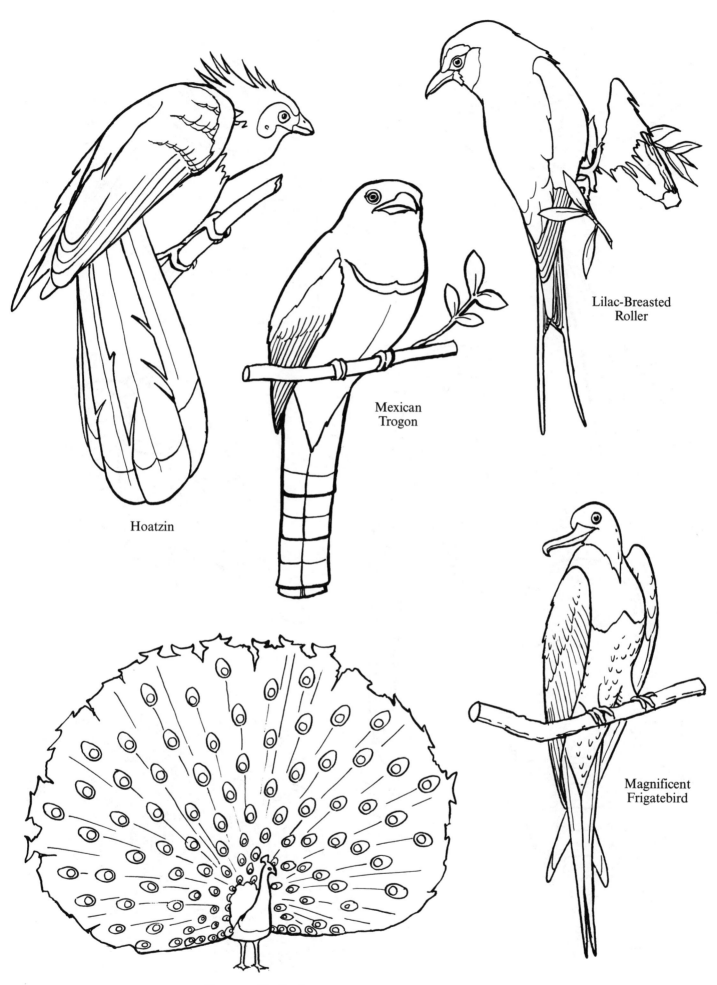

Hoatzin

Mexican
Trogon

Lilac-Breasted
Roller

Magnificent
Frigatebird

Common Peafowl

Greater Bird of Paradise

Green-Tailed Sylph

Regal Sunbird

Turquoise-Browed
Motmot

Cock-of-the-Rock

Tawny Frogmouth

Green Jay

White-Crested
Guan

Superb Lyrebird

Sulfur-Crested
Cockatoo

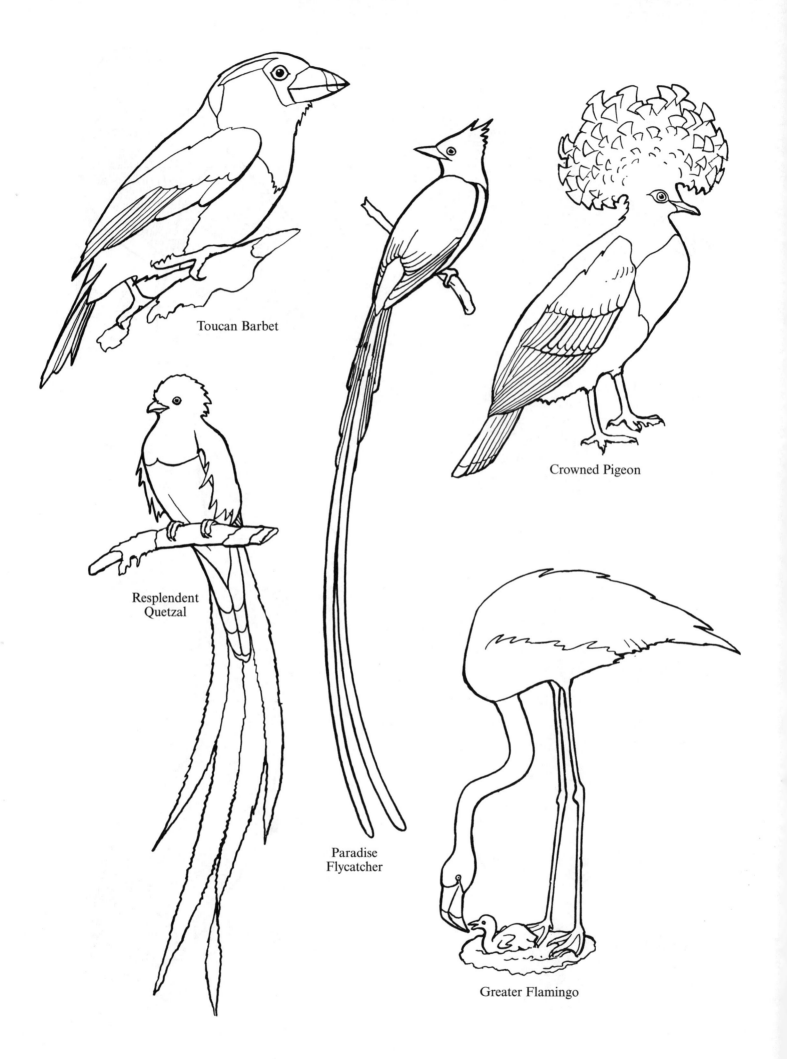

Toucan Barbet

Crowned Pigeon

Resplendent
Quetzal

Paradise
Flycatcher

Greater Flamingo

Common Pheasant

Wood Duck

Herring Gull

Bank Swallow

Osprey

Black-Capped Chickadee

Red-Tailed Hawk

Canada Goose

Piping Plover

Northern Harrier

Mute Swan

Yellow Warbler

Herring Gull

Common Yellowthroat

Exotic Chicken

Common Tern

Great Horned Owl

Snowy Egret

Belted
Kingfisher

Red-Breasted Goose

Crowned Crane

Brazilian
Tanager

Chajá

Wren

Condor

Crested
Curassow

Great Auk

Dipper

D'Albertis'
Bird of Paradise

Bee-Eater

Brush Turkey

Crowned Pigeon

Wandering
Albatross

Kiwi

American
Redstart

Wrybill

Ostrich

Cormorant

Common Heron

Ringed
Plover

Little Grebe

Pallas's Sand Grouse

Hawaii
Mamo

Umbrella
Bird

Treecreeper

Dodo

Nandu

Golden
Oriole

Leadbeater's
Cockatoo

Baltimore or
Northern
Oriole

Hamerkop

Tui

Land Rail

Seriemá

Goatsucker or Nightjar

Mistletoe
Thrush

Superb Lyrebird

Raven

Great
Tinamou

Skylark

Broadbill

Tooth-Billed
Pigeon

Scissor-Tailed
Flycatcher

Storm Petrel

Shoebill

Great
Titmouse

Plains Wanderer

Kagu

Green-Mantled
Turaco

Cuckoo

Ariel Toucan

Kakapo

Eastern Screech Owl

Indian Jaçana

Crested Pelican

Great Northern Diver

Hoatzin

White Stork

Weaver Bird

Roseate
Spoonbill

Plait-Billed
Hornbill

Satin Bowerbird

Common Tern

Great Bustard

Resplendent
Quetzal

Grey Parrot

Puffbird

Pitta

Northern
Gannet

Lämmergeier

Reed Pheasant

Frigatebird

Kirombo

Snow Bunting

Sunbittern

Common
Shelduck

Radiated
Ground-Cuckoo

Eurasian
Curlew

Bewick's Swan

Motmot

Long-Tailed
Hummingbird

Emu

Tody

Black-and-White
Warbler

Trumpeter

Greater Flamingo

Sugarbird

Great
Black-Headed
Gull

Purple Gallinule

Barn Owl

Secretary
Bird

Little Owl

Open-Billed
Stork

Coppersmith
Barbet

Rockhopper Penguin

Hazel Grouse

Lanner

Red-Faced Lovebird

Sunbittern

Ostrich

Smooth-Billed
Ani

Common Buzzard

Red-Legged
Partridge

Owl Parrot

Crested Grebe

Ptarmigan

Gray-Lag
Goose

Grand Potoo

Reeves'
Pheasant

Goshawk

Kaleege Pheasant

Crested Pigeon

Great Spotted
Cuckoo

Crested Curassow

Peacock Pheasant

California Quail

Stock
Pigeon

Ring Dove

Manakin

Red-Billed Jay

Ivory-Billed
Woodpecker

Piculet

Channel-Billed
Cuckoo

American Golden Plover

Silver Pheasant

African Trogon

Firetail

Cock-of-the-Rock

European Goosander

Crimson Tragopan

Serpent
Eagle

Rüppell's Vulture

Passenger
Pigeon

Tengmalm's Owl

Shoveler
Duck

Harpy Eagle

Concave-Casqued Hornbill

Boatbill

Motmot

White-Headed
Halcyon

Wandering Albatross

Marabou Stork

Ruff

Crowned Pigeon

Leschenault's
Forktail

Guiana Eagle

Eared Frogmouth

Whippoorwill

Ring Parrot

Rose-Crested
Cockatoo

European Kingfisher

Bohemian Waxwing

Three-Toed Woodpecker

Southern
Emuwren

Bruce's
Green Pigeon

Egyptian Goose

King Vulture

Seriemá

Nighthawk

Yellow-Billed
Cuckoo

Sand Grouse

Black Cockatoo

Double-Banded
Puffbird

Hoopoe

Long-Eared Owl

Hyacinthine Macaw

Shoebill

American Crow

Helmeted Guineafowl

Turkey Vulture

White-Tipped
Sicklebill

Marabou
Stork

Kookaburra

Tawny
Frogmouth

Common Teal

Glossy
Ibis

Burrowing
Owl

Chickadee

Harpy Eagle

White-Headed
Vulture

California Quail

Golden Eagle

Cuvier
Toucan

Brown
Violet-Eared
Hummingbird

Western
Bluebird

Downy
Woodpecker

Great Hornbill

Ostrich

Gila Woodpecker

Northern
Cardinal

House Sparrow

Northern
Cardinal

White-Throated
Sparrow

Northern Carmine
Bee-Eaters

Kori
Bustard

Ruby-Throated
Hummingbird

Imperial
Parrot

Sulfur-Breasted or
Keel-Billed Toucan

Red-Billed
Hornbill

Cactus Wren

Harris'
Hawk

Brown Kiwi

Baltimore or
Northern
Oriole

Northern
Mockingbird

Bee
Hummingbird

Buffon's
Macaw

Common Grackle

Secretary
Bird

Cedar
Waxwing

Prairie Hen

Bufflehead

Black-Bellied or
Gray Plover

American Golden Plover

Red-Eyed
Vireo

Booted
Eagle

Yellow-Breasted
Chat

Mississippi Kite

Eastern
Meadowlark

Virginia Quail

Vulturine
Sea-Eagle

Blue-Bearded
Bee-Eater

Pine Grosbeak

Bald Eagle

California
Condor

Cedar Bird

Carolina
Parakeet

Eastern Bluebird

Kirombo

Wild
Pigeon

Red-Bellied Woodpecker

Florida Burrowing Owl

Belted
Kingfisher

Goshawk

Black-Winged
Kite

Song
Sparrow

Abyssinian Ground-Hornbill

Forest
Woodhoopoe

Hawk-Billed
Parrot

Clapper Rail or
Marsh Hen

Turkey Vulture

Northern
Shrike

Yellow-Shafted Flicker

Wood Duck

Jamaica Tody

American
Wigeon

Short-Eared Owl

White-Eyed
Vireo

Great Horned Owl

Whistling Swan

Green
Parakeet

Eurasian Curlew

Bonelli's Eagle

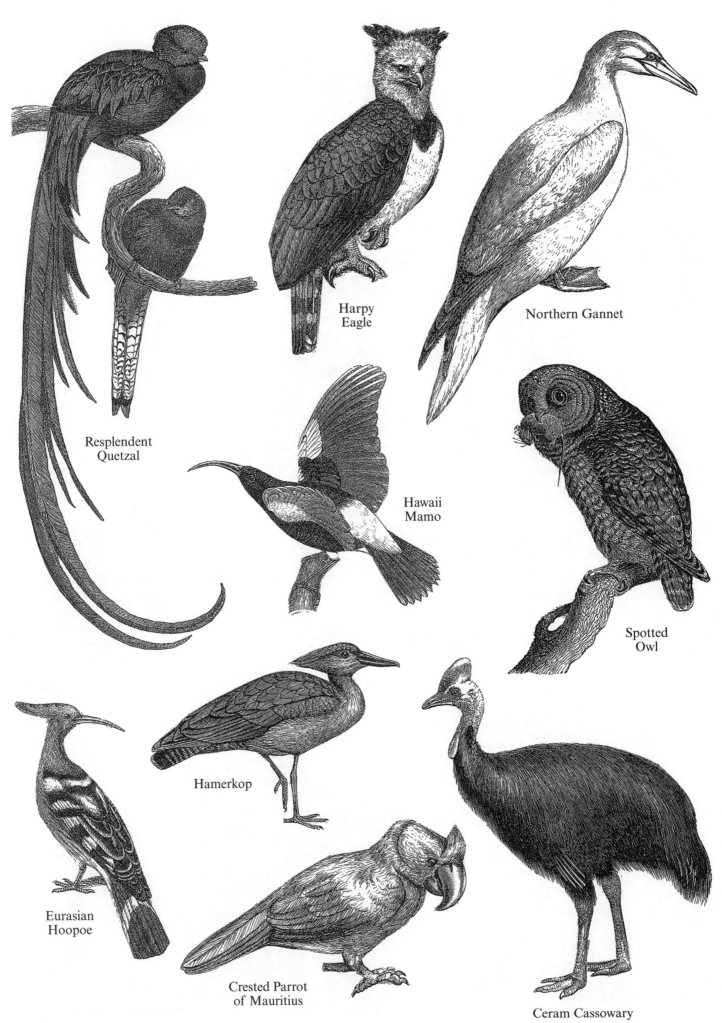

Resplendent
Quetzal

Harpy
Eagle

Northern Gannet

Hawaii
Mamo

Spotted
Owl

Hamerkop

Eurasian
Hoopoe

Crested Parrot
of Mauritius

Ceram Cassowary

Index of Scientific Names

Index of Common Names

Sources of the Illustrations

50 Favorite Birds Coloring Book, Lisa Bonforte
Copyright © 1982 Lisa Bonforte (ISBN: 0-486-24261-7)

Audubon's Birds of America Coloring Book, Paul E. Kennedy
Copyright © 1974 Dover Publications, Inc. (ISBN: 0-486-23049-X)

Birds of Prey Coloring Book, John Green
Copyright © 1989 John Green (ISBN: 0-486-25989-7)

State Birds and Flowers Coloring Book, Annika Bernhard
Copyright © 1990 Annika Bernhard (ISBN: 0-486-26456-4)

Hawaiian Plants and Animals Coloring Book, Y. S. Green
Copyright © 1999 Dover Publications, Inc. (ISBN: 0-486-40360-2)

Sea and Shore Birds Coloring Book, Ruth Soffer
Copyright © 1999 Ruth Soffer (ISBN: 0-486-40805-1)

Arctic and Antarctic Life Coloring Book, Ruth Soffer
Copyright © 1998 Dover Publications, Inc. (ISBN: 0-486-29893-0)

North American Ducks, Geese and Swans Coloring Book, Ruth Soffer
Copyright © 1996 Ruth Soffer (ISBN: 0-486-29165-0)

Swampland Animals Coloring Book, Ruth Soffer
Copyright © 1997 Dover Publications, Inc. (ISBN: 0-486-29625-3)

Tropical Birds Coloring Book, Lucia de Leiris
Copyright © 1984 Lucia de Leiris (ISBN: 0-486-24743-0)

Long Island Nature Preserves Coloring Book, Sy and Dot Barlowe
Copyright © 1997 Dover Publications, Inc. (ISBN: 0-486-29406-4)

Zoo Animals Coloring Book, Jan Sovak
Copyright © 1993 Dover Publications, Inc. (ISBN: 0-486-27735-6)

Backyard Nature Coloring Book, Dot Barlowe
Copyright © 1999 Dorothea Barlowe (ISBN: 0-486-40560-5)

Rain Forest Coloring Book, Annika Bernhard
Copyright © 1998 Annika Bernhard (ISBN: 0-486-40112-X)

Nocturnal Creatures Coloring Book, Ruth Soffer
Copyright © 1998 Ruth Soffer (ISBN: 0-486-40362-9)

African Plains Coloring Book, Dianne Gaspas-Ettl
Copyright © 1996 Dover Publications, Inc. (ISBN: 0-486-29230-4)

North American Desert Life Coloring Book, Ruth Soffer
Copyright © 1994 Dover Publications, Inc. (ISBN: 0-486-28234-1)

Birds, A. H. Evans, London, MacMillan & Co. Ltd., 1909.

The Standard Natural History, Vol. IV: *Birds,* ed. John Sterling Kingsley, Boston, S. E. Cassino & Co., copyright © 1885.

A Dictionary of Birds, Alfred Newton, London, Adam & Charles Black, 1893.

The New Natural History, Vol. IV, Richard Lydekker, New York, Merrill & Baker.

Key to North American Birds, Vol. II, Elliott Coues, Boston, Dana Estes & Co., 1903.

A Popular Handbook of the Ornithology of the United States and Canada, based on *Nuttall's Manual,* Vol. I: *The Land Birds,* Montague Chamberlain, Boston, Little, Brown, and Co., copyright © 1891